Dedication

This journal is dedicated to any person who is currently in foster care or previously in foster care.

I was in foster care myself as a young child. At times I felt abandoned, unwanted , confused and depressed. You may have experienced your own emotions.

I want you to know that you can get through this. I am a witness.

Use this journal to help you through the process, fill out the writing prompts, journal your thoughts and repeat the affirmations as much as you need to.

FOSTER 2 FOSTER

My life as a foster child

Rocking back and forth as I sit on the floor watching TV, bumping my head on the pillow as I nap. Sucking my thumb to give myself comfort. Saving my lunch to feed my brother and sister later. Always wanting to be the protector, always being the mother to my siblings.
What happened in my past?
Why am I saving food?
We eat everyday.
Why am I rocking and bumping my head, what trauma did I experience?
This is my life as a foster child.
However, I am not defined as a a foster child.
I am defined as God's child.
Foster care was the road I went down, but it helped lead me to my call.
To help others,
To bring hope and a future,
To be the change.

Michelle Anderson

DATE:

HOW HAS YOUR LIFE BEEN WHILE IN FOSTER CARE?

_____

_____

_____

_____

_____

_____

_____

_____

_____

_____

_____

_____

Who am I?

Who am I?
Who are you?
Who are we?
Some may say we are a throw away or
unwanted.
Some call me adopted,some call me a
foster child.
But, is that who we really are?
Am I who my mother says that I am, a
mistake?
How should I feel when she yells,
screams or throws things at me.
Wishing she never had me.
Am I who my father says that I am,
hardheaded?
Am I who my teacher says that I am,
bad and disrespectful?
Am I who my grandmother says that I
am, just average?
Who am I?
Am I like my mother, who makes
promises and don't keep them?

Am I like my father who wishes I were
never born?
I am not who my mother says that I
am, I am not who my father says that I
am.
I am who God says that I am.
I am not defined by my parents.
One day I went to church and the
pastor said that God called me to be
great.
I had never heard that before,
Me, great?
The pastor said that God wants me to
do something special.
I asked the pastor if I could take a
bible home and learn more.

I began to read more and more.
It said that I was chosen (John 15:16), that I was loved
(1 John 4:9-11), forgiven (1 John1:9) and had purpose
(Ephesians 2:10).
I am who God says that I am.
I am not ugly, unwanted or unloved.
I am not a mistake, God knew me before I was in my mothers
womb.
I finally know who I am and it is not a throw away.
I am chosen and wanted by God.
And so are you.

Michelle Anderson

Date:

Journal Entry

HOW I FEEL TODAY?

What if they told you?

What if they told you,
You are smart!
You are brilliant!
You can do all things with God on your side.
You are wonderfully made!
You are worth the wait!
What if they told you?
How would your life be different?
They never told me, so today I tell you
You are smart!
You are brilliant!
You can do all things and anything you put your mind
to!
You are wonderfully made and you are worth the
wait!
If nobody ever told you, today I tell you with
confidence.

Michelle Anderson

I am
Enough.

Date:

Journal Entry

WHAT HAPPENED TODAY?

I am Valuable.

DRAWING ACTIVITY

Date:

USE THIS SPACE TO DRAW A PICTURE OF HOW YOU FEEL TODAY.

A DAY IN MY LIFE FEELS LIKE...

Date:

Journal Entry

DO YOU THINK THAT IT IS YOUR
FAULT THAT YOU WENT TO
FOSTER CARE? WHY?

It is not my fault.

Date:

Journal Entry

WHAT HAPPENED TODAY?

I am not the mistakes of my parents.

Date:

Journal Entry

WHAT HAPPENED TODAY?

Date:

These are the things I will do this week if I start to feel lonely...

Date:

Journal Entry

WHAT HAPPENED TODAY?

DRAWING ACTIVITY

Date:

USE THIS SPACE TO DRAW A PICTURE OF A TIME YOU WERE HAPPY.

I have control of my thoughts. Nobody can control how I feel but me.

Date:

Journal Entry

WHAT HAPPENED TODAY?

I have control of my future.

Date:

Journal Entry

DRAWING ACTIVITY

Date:

USE THIS SPACE TO DRAW A PICTURE OF HOW YOU FEEL ON THE INSIDE.

Journal Entry

WHAT HAPPENED TODAY?

My past does not define me.

Journal Entry

HOW DO YOU BELIEVE YOUR PAST WILL AFFECT YOUR FUTURE?

The keys to my future is in my hands.

DRAWING ACTIVITY

Date:

USE THIS SPACE TO DRAW A PICTURE OF A TIME YOU WERE SAD.

Your feelings and actions do not define who you are...

You may feel angry but you are not an angry person.

You may make a mistake but you are not a mistake.

You may have bad thoughts, but that does not make you a bad person.

You may have had a bad grade but you are not stupid.

You may be different than other people but that makes you unique, not weird.

You may be in foster care but you are not unwanted.

Date:

Journal Entry

WHAT HAPPENED TODAY?

When I am angry I can...

Go to a quiet place. Close my eyes, take three deep breathes and think about a time I was happy.

Think about how I will make my future better than your past.

Write a list of three positive things.

When I am angry I can...

If you need to hit something, hit a pillow.

Listen to caliming music.

Do something physical, take a walk, jog in place or do stretches.

When I am angry I can...

Move away from what is making you angry.

Squeeze a ball or a stuffed
animal.

Write in your journal, write a letter about why you feel
angry or draw a picture.

Date ______________________

THINGS I WILL DO WHEN I AM ANGRY OR SAD

You choose your consequences, when you choose your actions.

-CURRENT FOSTER CARE WORKER

Date:

Journal Entry
WHAT HAPPENED TODAY?

I deserve to be loved.

Date:

Journal Entry

WHAT IS YOUR DEFINITION OF
LOVE?

I have Purpose.

Jeremiah 29:11 NIV
"For I know the plans I have for you, plans to prosper you and not to harm you, plans to give you hope and a future"

I am not A mistake.

JEREMIAH 1:5 "BEFORE I FORMED YOU IN THE WOMB I KNEW YOU, BEFORE YOU WERE BORN I SET YOU APART."

Date:

Journal Entry

Every family will not hurt you.

- FROM A FORMER FOSTER PARENT

Date:

Journal Entry

IF I COULD CHANGE ANYTHING IN MY LIFE, I WOULD CHANGE...

Psalms 139:13-14

For you created my inmost being; you knit me together in my mother's womb. I praise you because I am fearfully and wonderfully made; your works are wonderful, I know that full well.

One Day I Will

Date:

Journal Entry

DATE:

TODAY I WILL TELL MY STORY...

Date:

Journal Entry

WHAT HAPPENED TODAY?

I am capable
I am smart enough
I am brave enough
to do whatever I put
my mind to.

Date:

Journal Entry

WHAT HAPPENED TODAY?

These are the people I miss...

Date

Date:

Journal Entry

WHAT HAPPENED TODAY?

I am capable of accomplishing my goals.

_____
Date

Write a goal in each space and write down the steps to accomplishing them.

_____   _____
_____   _____
_____   _____
_____   _____
_____   _____
_____   _____
_____   _____
_____   _____
_____   _____

_____   _____
_____   _____
_____   _____
_____   _____
_____   _____
_____   _____
_____   _____
_____   _____

Date:

Journal Entry

One Day I Want To

Date:

Journal Entry

WHAT HAPPENED TODAY?

I am Forgiven.

Date:

Journal Entry

WHAT HAPPENED TODAY?

These are the people I will forgive...

Date _____

Date:

Journal Entry

WHAT HAPPENED TODAY?

I AM NOT A VICTIM, I AM VICTORIOUS

Date:

Journal Entry

WHAT HAPPENED TODAY?

Empower yourself to share your story.

- FROM A FORMER FOSTER CARE WORKER

TODAY I WILL TELL MY STORY...

DATE:

Date:

Journal Entry
WHAT HAPPENED TODAY?

There is life after foster care and you can be successful!

you can heal!

-MICHELLE ANDERSON
FORMER FOSTER CHILD

Journal Entry

Use the following pages for coloring, writing and drawing.

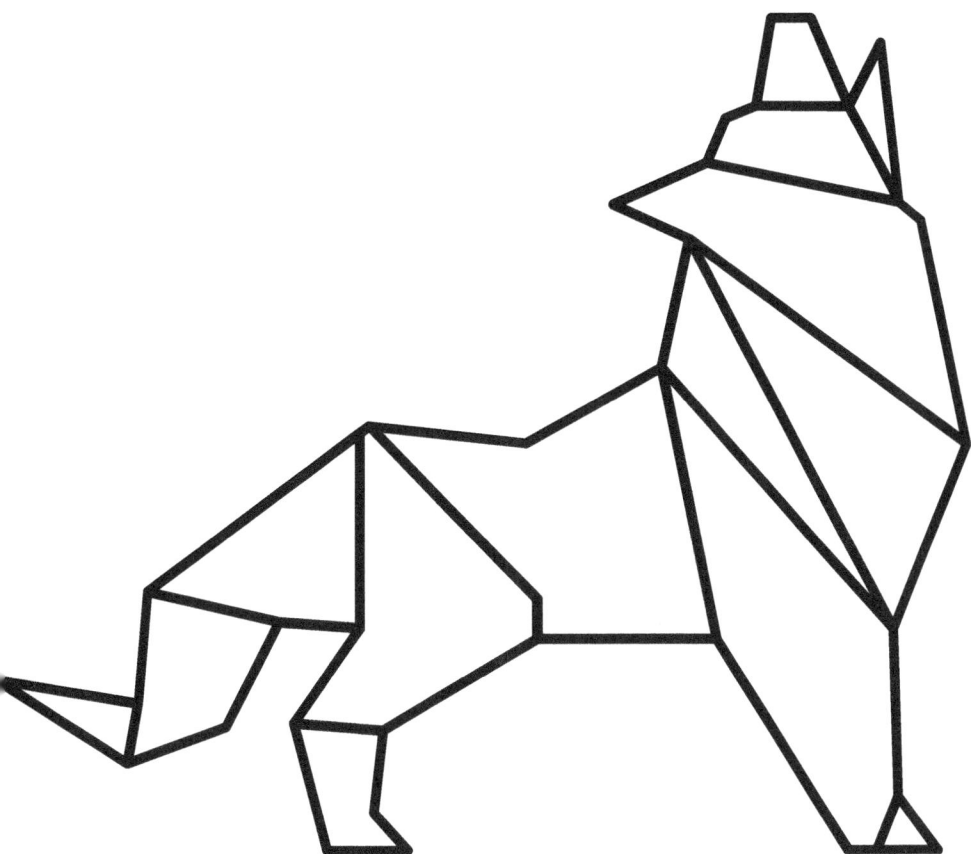

Your life matters.

You are stronger than you think.

Beauty lies within.

TODAY I CHOOSE JOY

Journal Entry

Date:

Journal Entry

Date:

Journal Entry

Foster2Foster
A Self-Guided Journal for children in foster care
Written by Michelle L. Anderson
Copyright © 2020
Cover Art by Maria Romain
All scripture taken from the Holy Bible
968-1-7355499-4-1
Published by Generations Soar LLC
www.generationssoar@gmail.com
Instagram: @generationssoar

www.ingramcontent.com/pod-product-compliance
Lightning Source LLC
Chambersburg PA
CBHW071820020426
42331CB00007B/1570